William Edward Hartpole Lecky

The Empire, its Value and its Growth

William Edward Hartpole Lecky

The Empire, its Value and its Growth

ISBN/EAN: 9783337267285

Printed in Europe, USA, Canada, Australia, Japan

Cover: Foto ©ninafisch / pixelio.de

More available books at **www.hansebooks.com**

THE EMPIRE

ITS VALUE AND ITS GROWTH

An Inaugural Address

DELIVERED AT THE IMPERIAL INSTITUTE, NOV. 20, 1893
UNDER THE PRESIDENCY OF H.R.H. THE PRINCE OF WALES

BY

W. E. H. LECKY

LONDON
LONGMANS, GREEN, AND CO.
AND NEW YORK : 15 EAST 16th STREET
1893

THE EMPIRE

ITS VALUE AND ITS GROWTH

—◦◦◦—

I HAVE been asked on the present occasion
to deliver a short address which might
serve as an introduction to the course of
lectures and conferences on the history
and resources of the different portions of
the Empire which are to take place in the
Imperial Institute. In attempting to dis-
charge this task my first reflection is one
which the very existence of the Institute
can hardly fail to suggest to anyone with
any knowledge of recent history. It is
the great revolution of opinion which has

taken place in England within the last few
years about the real value to her both of
her Colonies and of her Indian Empire.
Not many years ago it was a popular
doctrine among a large and important class
of politicians that these vast dominions
were not merely useless but detrimental
to the Mother-country, and that it should
be the end of a wise policy to prepare
and facilitate their disruption. James Mill,
who held a high place among these politicians, wrote an article on Colonies for
the 'Encyclopædia Britannica' which clearly
expresses their view. Colonies, he con-
tended, are very little calculated to yield
any advantage whatever to the countries
that hold them, and their chief influence is
to produce and prolong bad government.
Why, then, he asks, do European nations

maintain them ? The answer is very cha-
racteristic, both of the man and of his
school. Something, he charitably admits,
is due to mere ignorance, to mistaken
views of utility ; but the main cause is of
another kind. He quotes the saying of
Sancho Panza, who desired to possess an
island in order that he might sell its
inhabitants as slaves, and put the money
in his pocket ; and he maintains that the
chief cause of our colonial empire is the
selfish interest of the governing few who
valued colonies because they gave them
places and enabled them to multiply wars.
In more moderate and decorous language,
an eminent writer, who is still living,
wrote a book, the object of which was to
show how desirable it was that this empire
should be gradually but steadily reduced

to the sweet simplicity of two islands. Similar views prevailed very generally in the Manchester School. Cobden frequently expressed them. The question of the colonies, he maintained, was mainly a question of pounds, shillings, and pence; he proved, as he imagined, by many figures that they were a very bad bargain; and he expressed his confident hope that one of the results of Free-trade would be 'gradually and imperceptibly to loosen the bands which unite our colonies to us.' About our Indian Empire he entertained much stronger opinions. He described it as a calamity and a curse to the people of England. He looked on it, in his own words, 'with an eye of despair,' and declared that it was destroying and de-moralising the national character. It was the belief of his school of politicians that all the nations of the world would speedily follow the example of England and adopt a policy of perfect Free-trade ; that when all men were able to sell their industries with equal facility in all countries, it would become a matter of little consequence to them under what flag they lived, and that this complete commercial assimilation would soon be followed by a general movement for disarming, which would put an end to all fear of future war.

Many politicians who certainly cannot be classified with the Manchester School held views tending in some degree in the same direction. Even Sir Cornewall Lewis, in his treatise on the ' Government of Dependencies,' which was published in 1841, summed up the advantages and disad-

vantages of a great empire in a manner
that gives the impression that in his own
judgment the disadvantages on the whole
predominated. In the Autobiography of
that great writer and excellent public
servant, Sir Henry Taylor, who for many
years exercised much influence in the
Colonial Office, we have a curious picture
of the opinions which were held on this
subject about thirty years ago, both by
Henry Taylor himself and by Sir
Frederick Rogers, who was at this time
permanent Under-Secretary of State for
the Colonies. They both agreed that all
our North American Colonies were a kind
of *damnosa hereditas*, and that it was in
a high degree desirable that they should
be amicably separated from Great Britain.
Sir Henry Taylor wrote his views on the

subject with great frankness to the Duke of Newcastle, who was then Secretary of State. 'When your Grace and the Prince of Wales,' he said, 'were employing yourselves so successfully in conciliating the colonists, I thought that you were drawing closer ties which might better be slackened, if there were any chance of their slipping away altogether. I think that a policy which has regard to a not very far off future should prepare facilities and propensities for separation. . . . In my estimation the worst consequence of the late dispute with the United States has been that of involving this country and its North American provinces in closer relations and a common cause.'[1]

I do not believe that opinions of this

[1] *Autobiography,* ii. pp. 234, 235.

kind, though they were held by a large and powerful section of English politicians, ever penetrated very deeply into the English nation. One of the causes of Mr. Cobden's 'despair' was his conviction that the English people would never be persuaded to surrender India except at the close of a disastrous and exhausting war, and in his day the policy of national surrender was certainly not that of the statesmen who led either party in Parliament. No one would attribute it to Mr. Disraeli, in whose long political life the note of Imperialism was perhaps that which sounded with the clearest ring, and it was quite as repugnant to Lord Palmerston and Lord John Russell. In an admirable speech which was delivered in the beginning of 1850, Lord J. Russell disclaimed all sympathy with it, and I can well remember the indignation with which in his latter days he was accustomed to speak of the views on the subject which were then frequently expressed. ' When I was young,' he once said to me, ' it was thought the mark of a wise statesman that he had turned a small kingdom into a great empire. In my old age it appears to be thought the object of a statesman to turn a great empire into a small kingdom.'

I do not think that anyone who has watched the current of English opinion will doubt that the views of the Manchester School on this subject have within the last few years steadily lost ground, and that a far warmer and, in my opinion, nobler and more healthy feeling towards India and the colonies has grown up. The change may be attributed to many causes. In the first place, what Carlyle called ' The Calico Millennium ' has not arrived. The nations have not adopted Free-trade, but nearly all of them, including unfortunately many of our own colonies, have raised tariff walls against our trade. The Reign of Peace has not come. National antipathies and jealousies play about as great a part in human affairs as they ever did, and there are certainly not less than three and a half millions, there are probably nearly four millions, of men under arms in what are called the peace establishments of Europe. It is beginning to be clearly seen that, with our vast, redundant, ever-growing population, with our enormous manufactures, and our utterly insufficient supply of home-grown food, it is a matter of life and death to the nation, and especially to its working classes, that there should be secure and extending fields open to our goods, and in the present condition of the world we must mainly look for these fields within our own empire. The gigantic dimensions that Indian trade has assumed within the last few years, and the extraordinary commercial development of some other parts of our empire, have pointed the moral, and it has been made still more apparent by the eagerness with which other Powers, and especially Germany, have flung themselves into the path of colonisation. In an age, too, when all the paths of professional and industrial life in our country are crowded to excess. the competitive system has combined with our new acquisitions of territory to throw open noble fields of employment, enterprise and ambition to poor and struggling talent, and India is proving a school of inestimable value for maintaining some of the best and most masculine qualities of our race. It is the great seed-plot of our military strength ; and the problems of Indian administration are peculiarly fitted to form men of a kind that is much needed among us—men of strong purpose and firm will, and high ruling and organising powers, men accustomed to deal with facts rather than with words, and to estimate measures by their intrinsic value, and not merely by their party advantages, men skilful in judging human character under its many types and aspects and disguises.

If again we turn to our great self-governing colonies, we have learnt to feel

how valuable it is, in an age in which international jealousies are so rife, that there
should be vast and rapidly growing portions of the globe that are not only at
peace with us, but at one with us ; how
unspeakably important it is to the future
of the world that the English race, through
the ages that are to come, should cling as
closely as possible together. As the dis-
tinguished statesman who now represents
the United States in England lately said,
with an admirable point, If it is not
always true that trade follows flag, it is at
least true that ' heart follows flag,' and the
feeling that our fellow-subjects in distant
parts of the empire bear to us is very
different from the feeling even of the most
friendly foreign nation. Our great colonies
have readily undertaken the responsibility

of providing for their own defence by land, and even in some degree by sea. If the protection of their coast in time of war might become a great strain upon our navy, this disadvantage is largely balanced by the importance of distant maritime possessions to every nation that desires to maintain an efficient fleet ; by the immense advantage to a great commercial Power of secure harbours and coaling stations scattered over the world. It is not difficult to conceive circumstances in which the destruction of some of our main industries, occurring, perhaps, in the midst of a great war, might make it utterly impossible for our present population to live upon British soil, and when the possession of vast territories under the British flag, and in the hands of the

British race, might become a matter of transcendent importance. Think for a moment of the colossal, and indeed appalling, proportions which our great towns are assuming! Think of all the vice and ignorance and disease, of all the sordid abject misery, of all the lawless passions that are festering within them! And then consider how precarious are many of the conditions of our industrial prosperity, how grave and how numerous are the dangers that threaten it both from within and from without. Who can reflect seriously on these things without feeling that the day may come—perhaps at no distant date—when the question of emigration may overshadow all others? To many of us, indeed, it seems one of the greatest errors of modern English states-

B

manship that when the great exodus from
Ireland took place after the famine, Government took no step to aid it, or to direct
it to quarters where it would have been
of real benefit to the empire. Many
good judges think that the advantages of
such interference in allaying bitter feelings,
softening a disastrous crisis, and perma-
nently strengthening the empire, might
have been well purchased even if they cost
half or two-thirds as much as England
has lost in the last four months by
one disastrous strike. In dealing with
this question of emigration in the
future, colonial assistance may be of
supreme importance. And those who
have understood the significance of that
memorable incident in our recent history
—the despatch of Australian troops to

fight our battles in the Soudan—may perceive that there is at least a possibility of a still closer and more beneficent union between England and her colonies—a union that would vastly increase the strength of both, and by doing so become a great guarantee of peace in the world.

It would be a calumny to suppose that the change of feeling I have described was solely due to a calculation of interests. Patriotism cannot be reduced to a mere question of money, and a nation which has grown tired of the responsibilities of empire and careless of the acquisitions of its past and of its greatness in the future, would indeed have entered into a period of inevitable decadence. Happily we have not yet come to this. I believe the overwhelming majority of the people of these

islands are convinced that an England reduced to the limits which the Manchester
School would assign to it would be an
England shorn of the chief elements of its
dignity in the world, and that no greater
disgrace could befall them than to have sacri-
ficed through indifference, or negligence, or
faint-heartedness, an empire which has been
built up by so much genius and so much
heroism in the past. Railways and telegraphs and newspapers have brought us into closer touch with our distant possessions,
have enabled us to realise more vividly both
their character and their greatness, and
have thus extended the horizon of our
sympathies and interests. The figures of
illustrious colonial statesmen are becoming
familiar to us Men formed in Indian
and colonial spheres are becoming more

numerous and prominent in our own public life. The presence in England of a High Commissioner from Canada, and of Agents-General from our other colonies, constitutes a real though informal colonial representation, and on more than one recent occasion our foreign policy has been swayed by colonial pressure. These young democracies, with their vast undeveloped resources, their unwearied energies, their great social and industrial problems, are beginning to loom largely in the imaginations of Europe. They feel, we believe, a just pride in being members of a great and ancient empire, and heirs to the glories of its past. We, in our turn, feel a no less just pride in our union with those coming nations which are still lit with the hues of sunrise and rich in the promise of the future.

It has been suggested to me that I should on the present occasion say something about the methods by which this great empire was built up, but it is obvious that in a short address like the present it is only possible to touch on so large a subject in the most cursory manner.   Much is due to our insular position and our command of the sea, which gave Englishmen, in the competition of nations, a peculiar power both of conquering and holding distant dependencies.   Being precluded, perhaps quite as much by their position as by their desire, from throwing themselves, like most continental nations, into a long course of European aggression, they have largely employed their redundant energies in exploring, conquering, civilising, and governing distant and half-savage lands.   They have found, like all other nations, that an empire planted amid the shifting sands of half-civilised and anarchical races is compelled for its own security, and as a mere matter of police, to extend its borders. The chapter of accidents—which has played a larger part in most human affairs than many very philosophical enquirers are inclined to admit—has counted for something. But, in addition to these things, there are certain general characteristics of English policy which have contributed very largely to the success of the Empire.

It has been the habit of most nations to regulate colonial governments in all their details according to the best metropolitan ideas, and to surround them with a network of restrictions. England has in general pursued a different course. Partly on system, but partly also, I think, from neglect, she has always allowed an unusual latitude to local knowledge and to local wishes. She has endeavoured to secure, wherever her power extends, life and property, and contract and personal freedom, and, in these latter days, religious liberty ; but for the rest she has meddled very little ; she has allowed her settlements to develop much as they please, and has given, in practice if not in theory, the fullest powers to her governors. It is astonishing, in the history of the British Empire, how large a part of its greatness is due to the independent action of individual adventurers, or groups of emigrants, or commercial companies, almost wholly unassisted and uncontrolled by the Government at home. An empire formed by such methods is not likely to exhibit

much symmetry and unity of plan, but it
is certain to be pervaded in an unusual
degree, in all its parts, by a spirit of enterprise and self-reliance ; it will probably be
peculiarly fertile in men not only of energy
but of resource, capable of dealing with
strange conditions and unforeseen exi-
gencies. England in the past periods of
her history has, on the whole, been singularly successful in adapting her different administrations to widely different
national circumstances and characters, and
governments of the most various types
have arisen under her rule. Nothing in
the history of the world is more wonder-
ful than that under the flag of these two
little islands there should have grown
up the greatest and most beneficent des-
potism in the world, comprising nearly

two hundred and thirty millions of inhabitants under direct British rule, and more than fifty millions under British protectorates ; while at the same time British colonies and settlements that are scattered throughout the globe number not less than fifty-six distinct subordinate governments.

This system would have been less successful if it had not been for two important facts. The original stuff of which our colonial empire was formed was singularly good. Some of the most important of our colonies were founded in the days of religious war, and the early settlers consisted largely of religious refugees—a class who are usually superior to the average of men in intellectual and industrial qualities, and are nearly always greatly superior to them in strength of conviction, and in those high moral qualities which play so great a part in the well-being of nations. Besides this, in those distant days, the difficulties of emigration were so great that they were rarely voluntarily encountered except by men of much more than average courage, enterprise and resource. These early adventurers were certainly often of no saintly type, but they were largely endowed with the robuster qualities that are most needed for grappling with new circumstances and carving out the empires of the future.

The second fact is the high standard of patriotism and honour which we may, I think, truly say has nearly always prevailed among English public servants. It is not an easy thing to secure honest and faithful administration in remote countries, far from the supervision and practical control of the central government. I think we may boast with truth that England has attained this end, not indeed perfectly, but at least to a greater degree than most other nations. The history of Indian and colonial governors has never been written as a whole, but it is well worthy of study. In the appointment of these men party has always counted for something, and family has counted for something; but they have never been the only considerations, and, on the whole, I believe it will be found, if we consider the three elements of character, capacity and experience, that our Indian and colonial governors represent a higher level of ruling qualities than has been attained by any line of hereditary sovereigns, or by any line of elected presidents. In the period of the foundation of our Indian Empire much was done that was violent and rapacious, but the best modern research seems to show that the picture which a few years ago was generally accepted had been greatly overcharged. The history of Warren Hastings and his companions has been recently studied with great knowledge and ability, and with the result that the more serious opinions on the subject have been considerably modified. Much exaggeration undoubtedly grew up in the last century, partly through ignorance of Oriental affairs, and partly also through the eloquence of Burke. There is no figure in English political history for which I at least entertain a greater reverence than Edmund Burke. I believe him to have been a man of transparent honesty, as well as of transcendent genius ; but his politics were too apt to be steeped in passion, and he was often carried away by the irresistible force of his own imagination and feelings. Misrepresentations were greatly consolidated by the Indian History of James Mill, which was for a long time the main, and indeed almost the only, source from which Englishmen obtained their knowledge of Indian history. It was written, as might be expected, with the strongest bias of hostility to the English in India, yet I suspect that many superficial readers imagined that a history which was so unquestionably dull must be at least impartial and philosophical. Unfortunately, Macaulay relied greatly on it, and, without having made any serious independent studies on the subject, he invested some of its misrepresentations with all the splendour of his eloquence. I believe all competent authorities are now agreed that his essay on Warren Hastings, though it is one of the most brilliant of his writings, is also one of the most seriously misleading.

I am not prepared to say that the reaction of opinion produced by the new school of Indian historians has not been sometimes carried too far, but these writers have certainly dispelled much exaggeration and some positive falsehood. They have shown that, although, under circumstances of extreme difficulty and extraordinary temptation, some very bad things were done by Englishmen in India, these things were neither as numerous nor as grave as has been alleged.

On the whole, too, it may be truly said that English colonial policy in its broad lines has to a remarkable degree avoided grave errors. The chief exception is to be found in the series of mistakes which produced the American Revolution, and ended in the loss of our chief American Colonies. Yet even in this instance it is, I believe, coming to be perceived that there is much more to be said for the English case than the historians of the last generation were apt to imagine. In imposing commercial restrictions on the colonies we merely acted upon ideas that were then almost universally received, and our commercial code was on the whole less illiberal than that of other nations. This has been

clearly shown by more than one writer on
our side of the Atlantic, but the subject
has never been treated with more ex-
haustive knowledge and more perfect
impartiality than by an American writer—
Mr. George Beer—whose work on the
Commercial Policy of England has
recently been published by Columbia
College, in New York. No one will now
altogether defend Grenville's policy of tax-
ing America by the Imperial Parliament,
but it ought not to be forgotten that it
was expressly provided that every farthing
of this taxation was to be expended in
America, and devoted to colonial defence.
England had just terminated a great war,
which, by expelling the French from
Canada, had been of inestimable advantage
to her colonies, but which had left the

C

mother-country almost crushed by debt.
All that Grenville desired was, that the
American Colonies should provide a por-
tion of the cost of their own defence, as our
great colonies are doing at the present time,
and he only resorted to Imperial taxation
because he despaired of achieving this end
by any other means. The step which he
took was no doubt a false one. As is so often
the case in England, it was made worse by
party changes and by party recriminations,
and many later mistakes aggravated and
embittered the original dispute ; but I think
an impartial reader of this melancholy
chapter of English history will come to the
conclusion that these mistakes were by no
means all on one side.

It is a story which is certainly not
without its lesson to our own time. It

is very improbable that any future statesman will follow the example of George
Grenville, and endeavour by Act of Parliament to impose taxation on a self-
governing colony ; but it would be a grave
error to suppose that the danger of unwise
Parliamentary interference in Indian and
colonial affairs has diminished. Great
as are the advantages of telegraphs
and newspapers in the government of the
empire, they are not without their draw-
backs. Government by telegraph is a very
dangerous thing, and there is, I fear, an in-
creasing tendency to override local knowledge, and to apply English standards and
methods of government to wholly un-
English conditions. Ill-considered resolu-
tions of the House of Commons, often
passed in obedience to some popular fad,

and without any real intention of carrying them into effect ; language used in Parliament which is often due to no deeper motive than a desire to win the favour of some class of voters in an English constituency, may do as much as serious misgovernment to alienate great masses of British subjects beyond the sea. All really competent judges are agreed that one of the first conditions of successful government in India has been that Indian questions have for the most part been kept out of the range of English party politics, and that Indian government has been conducted on principles essentially different from democratic government at home.

On the whole, however, it is impossible to review the colonial history of England without being struck with the many serious dangers that might easily have shattered the empire, which were averted by wise statesmanship and timely concession. There was the question of the criminal population which we once transported to Australia. In the early stage of the colony, when the population was very sparse and the need for labour very imperative, this was not regarded as in any degree a grievance ; but the time came when it became a grievance of the gravest kind, and the Imperial power had then the wisdom to abandon it. There was the question of the different and hostile religious bodies existing in different portions of the empire, at a time when the monopoly of political power by the members of a single Established Church was cherished as a religious duty by politicians at home. Yet at this very time the Imperial Government sanctioned in Canada, and in some other parts of its dominions, a system of dealing with dissenting Churches far more liberal than that which it admitted in these islands, while in India it abstained, with an extreme, and sometimes even an exaggerated, scrupulousness, from all measures that could by any possibility offend the native religious prejudices. There was the question of Slavery—though we were freed from the most difficult part of this problem by the secession of America. In addition, however, to its moral aspects, it affected most vitally the material prosperity of some of our richest colonies ; it raised the very dangerous constitutional question of the right of the Imperial Parliament to interfere with the internal affairs of a self-governing colony, and it brought the Home Government into more serious collision with the local governments than any question since the American Revolution. Whatever may be thought of the wisdom of the measures by which we abolished slavery in our West Indian Colonies, no one at least can deny the liberality of a Parliament which voted from Imperial resources twenty millions for the accomplishment of the work. There was the conflict of race and creed which between 1830 and 1840 had brought Canada to absolute rebellion, and threatened a complete alienation of Canadian feeling from the mother-country. This discontent was allayed and dispelled by some of the most

successful legislation of the present century, and in spite of a few discordant
notes, it may be truly said that there
are few greater contrasts in the present
reign than are presented between Canadian
feeling towards the mother-country when
Her Majesty ascended the throne and
Canadian feeling at the present hour.   There
was also the great and dangerous task to
be accomplished of adapting the system of
colonial government to the different stages
of colonial development.   There was a time
when the colonies were so weak that they
depended mainly on England for their protection ; but, unlike some of the great colon-
ising Powers of ancient and modern times,
England never drew a direct tribute from
her colonies, and, in spite of much unwise
and some unjust legislation, I believe there

was never a time when they were not on
the whole benefitted by the connection.
Soon, however, the colonies grew to the
strength and maturity of nationhood, and
the mother-country speedily recognised
the fact, and allowed no unworthy or un-
generous fears to restrain her from granting
them the fullest powers, both of self-govern-
ment and of federation.   It is true that she
still sends out a governor—usually drawn
from the ranks of experienced and considerable English public men—to preside
over colonial affairs.   It is true that she
retains a right of veto which is scarcely
ever exercised except to prevent some inter-
colonial or international dispute, some act
of violence, or some grave anomaly in the
legislation of the empire.   It is true that
colonial cases may be carried, on appeal, to

an English tribunal, representing the very highest judicial capacity of the mother-country, and free from all possibility and suspicion of partiality ; but I do not believe that any of these light ties are un-popular with any considerable section of the colonists. On the other hand, though it would be idle to suppose that our great colonies depend largely upon the mother-country, I believe that most colonists recognise that there is something in the weight and dignity attaching to fellow-membership and fellow-citizenship in a great empire—something in the protection of the greatest navy in the world—something in the improved credit which con-nection with a very rich centre undoubtedly gives to colonial finance.

It is the custom of our friends and

neighbours on the Continent to bestow much scornful remark on the egotism of English policy, which attends mainly to the interests of the British Empire, and is not ready to make war for an idea and in support of the interests of others. I think, if it were necessary, we might fairly defend ourselves by showing that in the past we have meddled with the affairs of other nations quite as much as is reasonable. For my own part, I confess that I distrust greatly these explosions of military bene-volence. They always begin by killing a great many men. They usually end in ways that are not those of a disinterested philan-thropy. After all, an egotism that mainly confines itself to the well-being of about a fifth part of the globe cannot be said to be of a very narrow type, and it is essentially by her conduct to her own empire that the part of England in promoting the happiness of mankind must be ultimately judged. It is indeed but too true that many of the political causes which have played a great part on platforms, in parties, and in Parliaments are of such a nature that their full attainment would not bring relief to one suffering human heart, or staunch one tear of pain, or add in any appreciable degree to the real happiness of a single home. But most assuredly imperial questions are not of this order. Remember what India had been for countless ages before the establishment of British rule. Think of its endless wars of race and creed, its savage oppressions, its fierce anarchies, its barbarous customs, and then consider what it is to have established for so many years

over the vast space from the Himalayas to
Cape Comorin a reign of perfect peace ; to
have conferred upon more than 250 millions
of the human race perfect religious freedom,
perfect security of life, liberty, and property ;
to have planted in the midst of these teem-
ing multitudes a strong central government, enlightened by the best knowledge of
Western Europe, and steadily occupied in
preventing famine, alleviating disease, ex-
tirpating savage customs, multiplying the
agencies of civilisation and progress. This,
gentlemen, is the true meaning of that
system of government on which Mr.
Cobden looked with ' an eye of despair.'
What work of human policy—I would
even say what form of human philanthropy
—has ever contributed more largely to
reduce the great sum of human misery

and to add to the possibilities of human happiness ?

And if we turn to the other side of our empire, although it is quite true that our great free colonies are fully capable of shaping their destinies for themselves, may we not truly say that these noble flowers have sprung from British and from Irish seeds ? May we not say that the laws, the constitutions, the habits of thought and character that have so largely made them what they are, are mainly of English origin ? May we not even add that it is in no small part due to their place in the British Empire that these vast sections of the globe, with their diverse and sometimes jarring interests, have remained at perfect peace with us and with each other, and have escaped the curse of an exaggerated militarism, which is fast eating like a canker into the prosperity of the great nations of Europe ?

What may be the future place of these islands in the government of the world no human being can foretell. Nations, as history but too plainly shows, have their periods of decay as well as their periods of growth. The balance of power in the world is constantly shifting. Maxims and influences very different from those which made England what she is are in the ascendent, and the clouds upon the horizon are neither few nor slight. But, whatever fate may be in store for these islands, we may at least confidently predict that no revolution in human affairs can now destroy the future ascendency of the English language and of the Imperial race. Whatever misfortunes, whatever humiliations, the future may reserve to us, they cannot deprive England of the glory of having created this mighty empire.

Not Heaven itself upon the Past has power.
That which has been, has been—and we have had our
    hour.

PRINTED BY
SPOTTISWOODE AND CO., NEW STREET SQUARE
LONDON